Animals from Head to Tail

PIGS FROM HEAD TO TAIL

I0797553

By Emmett Martin

Please visit our website, www.garethstevens.com. For a free color catalog of all our high-quality books, call toll free 1-800-542-2595 or fax 1-877-542-2596.

Library of Congress Cataloging-in-Publication Data

Names: Martin, Emmett, author.
Title: Pigs from head to tail / Emmett Martin.
Description: New York : Gareth Stevens Publishing, [2021] | Series: Animals from head to tail | Includes index.
Identifiers: LCCN 2019042315 | ISBN 9781538255407 (library binding) | ISBN 9781538255384 (paperback) | ISBN 9781538255391 (6 pack) | ISBN 9781538255414 (ebook)
Subjects: LCSH: Swine–Juvenile literature.
Classification: LCC SF395.5 .M37 2021 | DDC 636.4–dc23
LC record available at https://lccn.loc.gov/2019042315

First Edition

Published in 2021 by
Gareth Stevens Publishing
111 East 14th Street, Suite 349
New York, NY 10003

Editor: Therese Shea
Designer: Laura Bowen

Photo credits: Cover, p. 1 acceptphoto/Shutterstock.com; p. 5 John Burke/The Image Bank/Getty Images Plus/Getty Images; p. 7 Peter Muller/Cultura/Getty Images; p. 9 andresr/E+/Getty Images; p. 11 bruev/iStock/Getty Images Plus/Getty Images; p. 13 ALEAIMAGE/E+/Getty Images; pp. 15, 24 (snout) Waltraud Herbert-Klemm/EyeEm/EyeEm/Getty Images; p. 17 Alan_Lagadu/E+/Getty Images; pp. 19, 24 (tusk) Ann & Steve Toon/robertharding/Getty Images Plus/Getty Images; p. 21 Photofusion/Contributor/Universal Images Group Editorial/Getty Images; p. 23 Byrdyak/iStock/Getty Images Plus/Getty Images.

Printed in the United States of America

CPSIA compliance information: Batch #CS20GS: For further information contact Gareth Stevens, New York, New York at 1-800-542-2595.

Contents

Some pigs are small.
Some are very big!

Some pigs live on farms.
Some are wild.

Some pigs are pets.
Pigs are smart!

Pigs have fat bodies and short legs.

They have hair
on their skin.

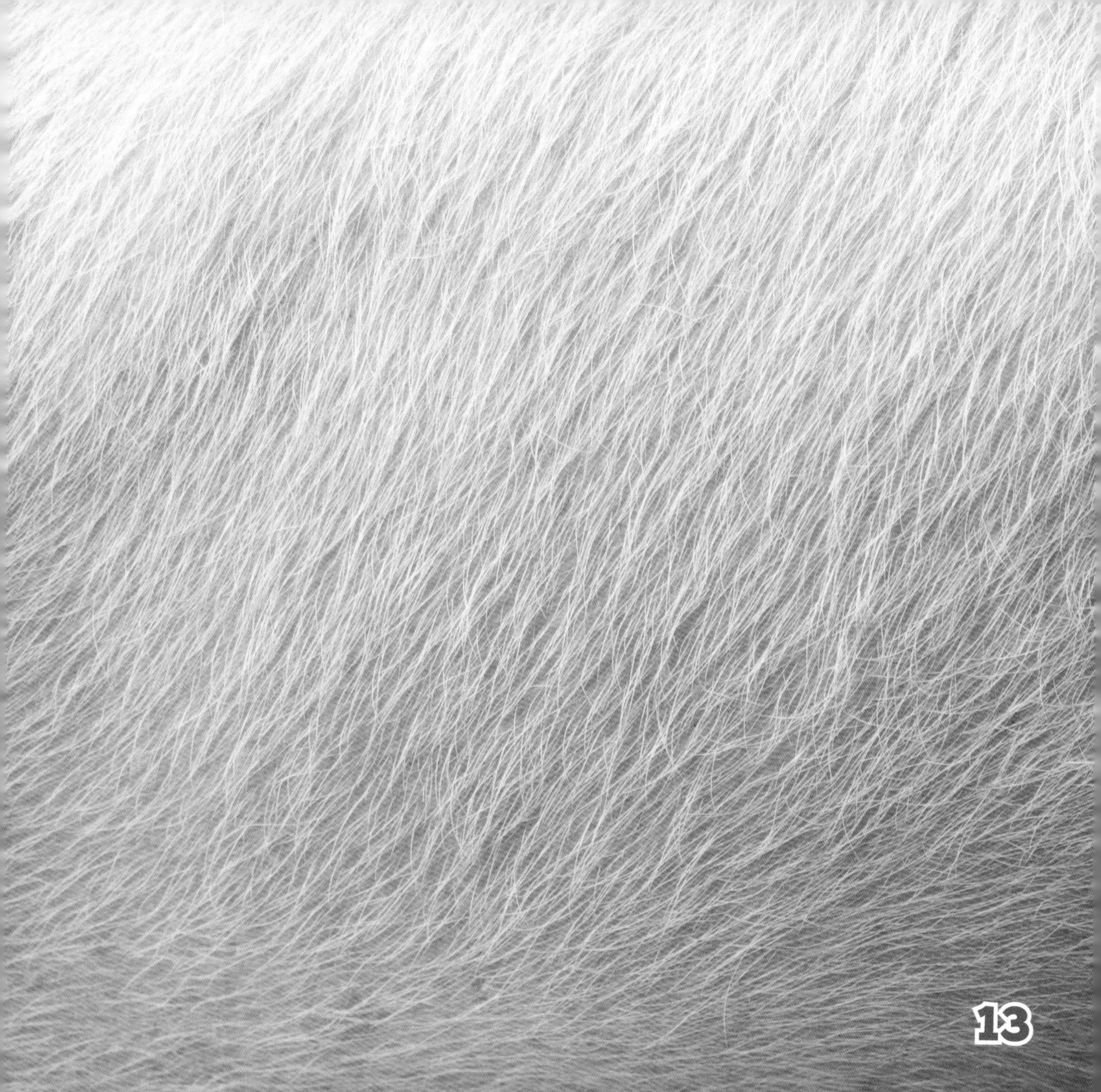

A pig's nose is its snout.
The snout is round
and flat.

Pigs have tails.
Some tails are curly.
Some are straight.

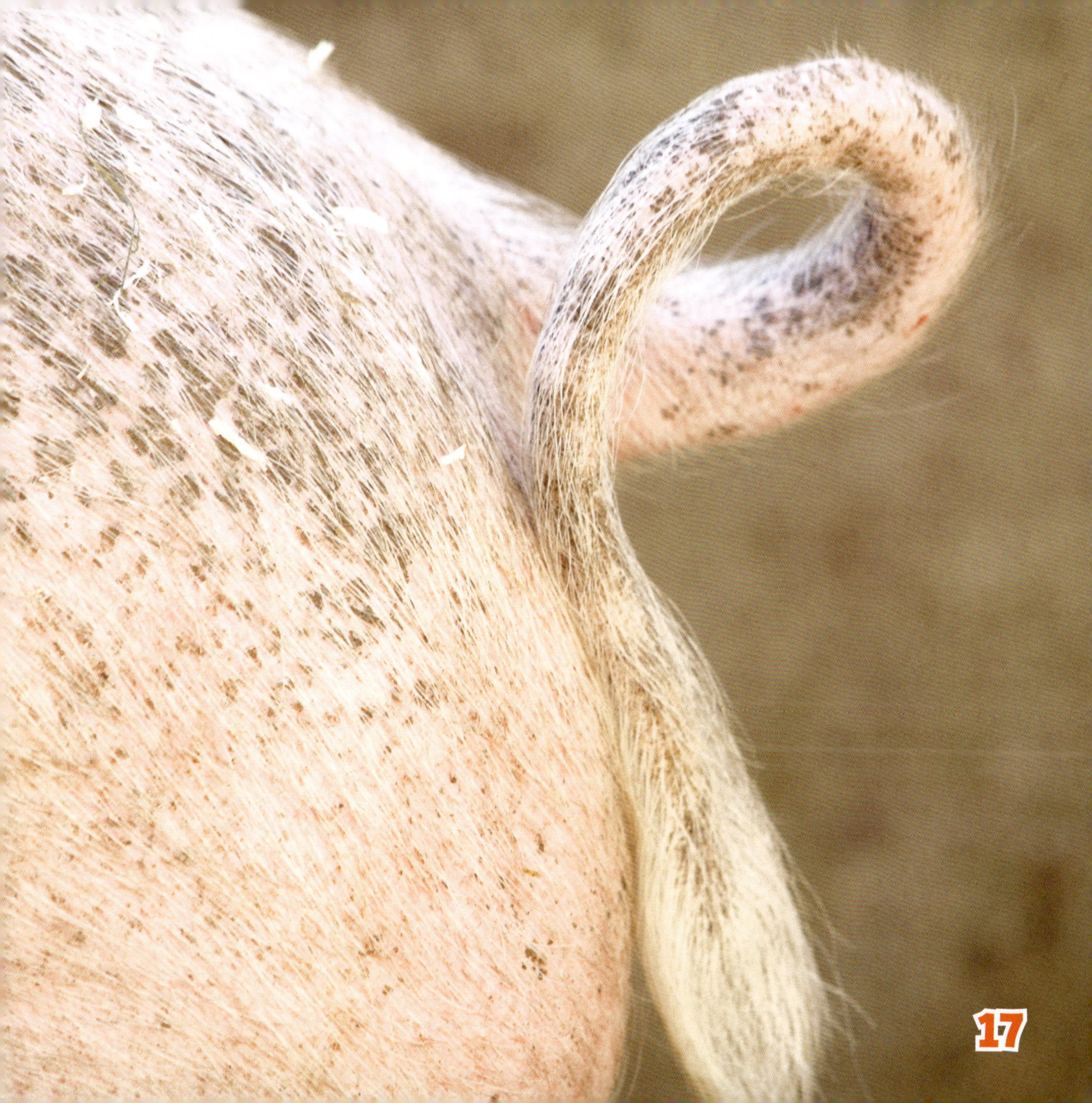

All pigs have teeth.
Wild pigs have
sharp tusks.

Pigs lay in mud
to keep cool.

Pigs have babies called piglets!

Words to Know

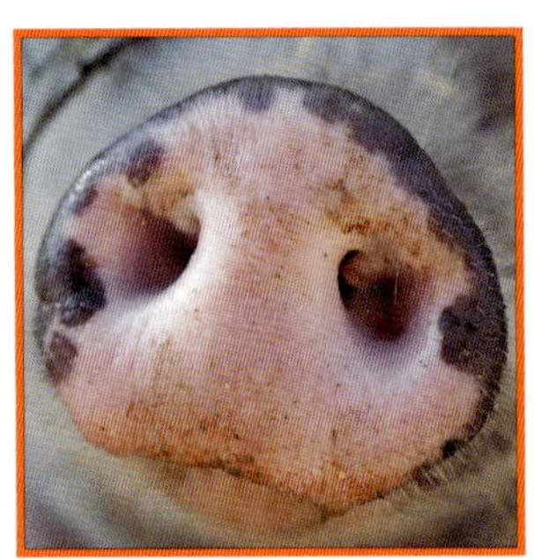

snout

tusk

Index